OFF THE BEATEN TRACK

A Guide to Mountain Biking in North Georgia

Volume III

Jim Parham

TABLE OF CONTENTS

THE TRAILS

Off the Beaten Track

Volume III:
North Georgia

Jim Parham

WMC
Publishing

Also by Jim Parham:

OFF THE BEATEN TRACK
Volume I: A Guide to Mountain Biking
in Western North Carolina

OFF THE BEATEN TRACK
Volume II: A Guide to Mountain Biking
in Western North Carolina—
Pisgah National Forest

49 Fun & Inexpensive
Things To Do In The Smokies
With Children

INTRODUCTION

For all practical purposes, the southern end of the Appalachian Mountain Range begins in the northern portion of Georgia. This end of the chain is called the Blue Ridge. Starting as mere foothills, these southern mountains rise to over 4,000 feet before spreading into North Carolina, Tennessee, and northward all the way to Canada.

These are old mountains. At 230 million years, they are the oldest in North America. Rounded off by time and covered with lush vegetation, from a distance they appear gentle and smooth. Once in their heart, however, you'll find them as rugged as they come, complete with waterfalls, cliffs, and gorges. There is wildlife here too. If you're lucky, you may spot a deer, a turkey, or even a bear.

Interspersed in these hills is a network of mountain roads and single track trails perfect for mountain biking. Most are within the Chattahoochee National Forest and all are well maintained.

You'll find dirt roads that snake up the valleys and traverse the highest ridges. Some have gates to keep motor vehicles out, while others are so lightly traveled it's rare to see a car. Also here is an assortment of single track trails designated for mountain bike use. On these you can travel into remote gorges, along precipitous mountain tops, and through dense forests. While some are steep, rocky, and tortuous, others are smooth and fast. Several were developed and are maintained by the Southern Off Road Bicycling Association (SORBA). We owe this organization many thanks.

By taking these trails and roads and linking them together, I've created quite an assortment of bicycling routes to choose from. They all start and finish at the same place and most form loops. I've also included in some of the routes sections of paved roads. I find these to be a pleasant contrast to the gravel roads and trails and good alternatives in wet weather. On some rides you come crashing out from harsh mountain terrain onto a gentle paved road which leads into a quiet, peaceful valley surrounded by mountains. On others, you may coast for miles down a steep, smooth, paved mountainside before exiting on some hidden trail.

One of the best things about mountain biking in North Georgia is that it is a year-round activity. Although a few winter days can be quite cold, most are not too cold and snow is rare. Summer days are hot, but once in the shade of the mountains, you'll find riding to be very pleasant. Of course in spring and fall the temperatures are almost always perfect.

With the changes of season, so change the type of users you are likely to see while out on the trail. In summer you'll encounter tourists of all kinds. Most come to escape the heat of the deep south. They may be hiking, fishing, camping, tubing in the creek, horseback riding or biking, like yourself. As the leaves begin to show off their brilliance in the fall, the number of cars with "leaf lookers" inside picks up on the secondary roads. Give them a wide berth as they tend to be looking up most of the time. Late fall and through the winter is hunting season, so be prepared to see people with guns in the woods. It may be prudent to wear brightly colored clothing at this time. You'll find spring to be the quietest, and perhaps the most beautiful months of all. Keep in mind also that the Chattahoochee is a multiple use forest, so expect at any time to see loggers opening up new tracts of land to timber harvesting or maintenance crews building and repairing roads.

I think you will be drawn to these mountains again and again for the great riding. Whether you are a seasoned expert or a first time mountain biker, there are plenty of great trails to choose from. Most can be done in half a day or less. I've rated the routes at three different levels: easiest, more difficult, and most difficult. Keep in mind that these ratings are relative to this book and to the topography of North Georgia. You'll find the most difficult trails here not quite as demanding as the most difficult routes listed in *Volume II* of this series which describes trails in North Carolina's Pisgah National Forest. This is not to say they are in any way easy. It's best not to overestimate your ability level and to pay close attention to the time allowances I've given to get the most enjoyment out of every ride. Also, for simplicity, I've provided all the information you need for a ride on two facing pages. This way there's no frustration flipping back and forth between pages while you are trying to figure out where you are on the map. You might even want to make a copy of the directions before you leave, so as not to have to carry the entire book on each ride.

Exploring these routes is a lot of fun. I hope you will enjoy them as much as I do.

J.P.
November, 1993

How To Use This Book

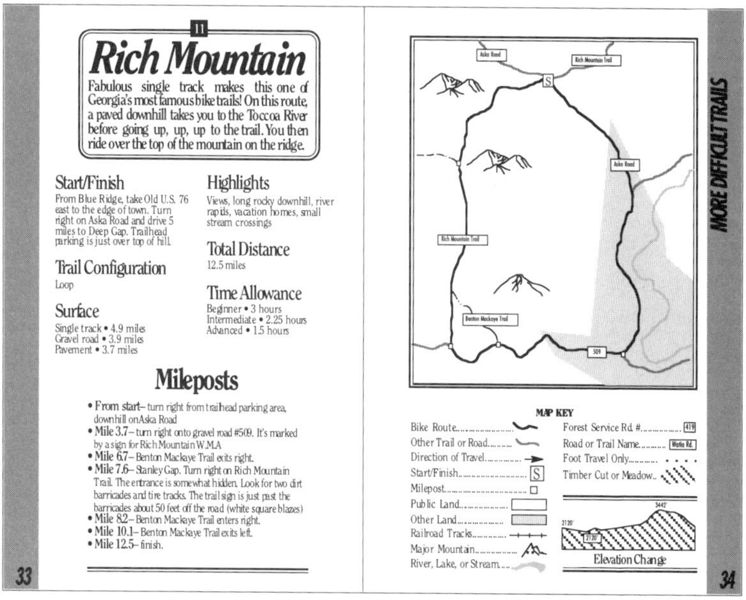

11

Rich Mountain

Fabulous single track makes this one of Georgia's most famous bike trails! On this route, a paved downhill takes you to the Toccoa River before going up, up, up to the trail. You then ride over the top of the mountain on the ridge.

Start/Finish
From Blue Ridge, take Old U.S. 76 east to the edge of town. Turn right on Aska Road and drive 5 miles to Deep Gap. Trailhead parking is just over top of hill.

Trail Configuration
Loop

Surface
Single track • 4.9 miles
Gravel road • 3.9 miles
Pavement • 3.7 miles

Highlights
Views, long rocky downhill, river rapids, vacation homes, small stream crossings

Total Distance
12.5 miles

Time Allowance
Beginner • 3 hours
Intermediate • 2.25 hours
Advanced • 1.5 hours

Mileposts

- From start– turn right from trailhead parking area, downhill on Aska Road
- Mile 3.7– turn right onto gravel road #509. It's marked by a sign for Rich Mountain W.M.A
- Mile 6.7– Benton Mackaye Trail exits right.
- Mile 7.6– Stanley Gap. Turn right on Rich Mountain Trail. The entrance is somewhat hidden. Look for two dirt barricades and tire tracks. The trail sign is just past the barricades about 50 feet off the road (white square blazes)
- Mile 8.2– Benton Mackaye Trail enters right.
- Mile 10.1– Benton Mackaye Trail exits left.
- Mile 12.5– finish.

33

Aska Road
Rich Mountain Trail
S
Aska Road
Rich Mountain Trail
Benton Mackaye Trail
509
MORE DIFFICULT TRAILS
MAP KEY
Bike Route
Other Trail or Road
Direction of Travel
Start/Finish
Milepost
Public Land
Other Land
Railroad Tracks
Major Mountain
River, Lake, or Stream
Forest Service Rd. #
Road or Trail Name
Foot Travel Only
Timber Cut or Meadow
3442'
2120'
Elevation Change
34

Typical Route Description Page

- The **route number** appears in either a circle, a square, or a diamond at the top of the left hand page. The number corresponds to the route number in the table of contents, and the circle (easiest), square (more difficult), or diamond (most difficult) indicates the route difficulty.

- **Route difficulty** (also shown vertically at the edge of the top right hand corner of the right page) is relative to this book and the North Georgia mountains. Although these mountains are not quite as high or as extreme as those further to the north, you can expect to find difficulties of every kind, including long, steep uphills and downhills, stream crossings, and plenty of rocky, technical single track.

- Below the **route name** is a brief description of the route's more noted highlights.

- **Start/Finish** indicates where the route begins and how to get there.

- **Trail Configuration** describes the type of route.

- There are three **Surface** types: single track, gravel road, and pavement. This shows how many miles to expect of each surface.

- In the **Highlights** there will be a one- or two-word description of things you can expect on the trail. For example, *ATV use* means: use caution; you may encounter all-terrain vehicles coming from either direction and you can expect the trail to show considerable wear and tear.

- The **Total Distance** shows the number of miles you will travel.

- **Time Allowance** is a rough approximation of the time it will take you to ride the trail with *minimal* stops according to your ability level.

- Each **Milepost** corresponds to the adjoining map. The first milepost is at the Start/Finish and is represented by a ⑤ on the map. There is a milepost for every turn or any other place of note and each is represented by a ▢ on the map.

- The **maps** are oriented north with all roads or trails marked by name or number. All roads, trails, buildings, clearings, and other features relevant to the route are shown, as well as the best direction of travel. Some of the routes listed in this book can be linked together for shorter or longer rides. When this is the case, those trails or roads are also shown on the map. However, no mileposts or directions are given for these combined rides. **Maps are not drawn to scale.**

- The **Map Key** shows what each symbol represents as well as indicating the shading used for different types of trails, roads, or land. The main route is always shown in black.

- By looking at the **Elevation Change**, you can get a pretty good idea where the major hills are in the route, how long they will be, and the degree of steepness. It does not show every short rise or dip in the trail.

Other Sections

- There are two sections immediately following this page that cover **Mountain Bike Etiquette** and **Riding In The Chattahoochee National Forest**. Knowing and following the rules and using good judgement is critical in keeping public land available to mountain bikers.

- On the **Orientation Pages** you'll find a map showing where the riding region is as it relates to the rest of Georgia and an area map indicating where you'll find the start/finish for each route.

- In the **Regional Information** section are several subsections that provide information on places to stay in the area, where bike shops are located, and what kind of weather and temperatures you can expect at different times of the year.

Mountain Bike Etiquette

The old phrase "use it or lose it"has never been more true than in the case of mountain biking on public and private lands. In this case it's more appropriate to say "use it *properly* or lose it." It takes only a few incidents of irresponsible or abusive trail riding to close a trail, a recreation area, or an entire national forest to mountain bikers. Below is a list of guidelines to follow while on the trail.

- Ride only on roads and trails authorized for mountain bike use. Some trails are only open at certain times of the year and others do not permit mountain bike use at all.

- To avoid trail erosion, carry your bike over wet and boggy areas, stepping stones, and steps. Also avoid skidding or spinning out on steep grades.

- Control your speed and approach turns in anticipation of someone around the bend.

- Always wear your helmet.

- Pack out what you pack in.

- Follow the directions of the "yield to" sign shown below. Dismount and be courteous to all other trail users when approaching from behind or ahead and make your presence known well in advance. If you meet horseback riders, speak out in a normal voice while they pass. This calms both the horses and their riders.

Riding in the Chattahoochee National Forest

The Chattahoochee National Forest in Georgia is finely suited to the sport of mountain biking. Many trails and miles upon miles of well maintained service roads are found within its borders. These roads are well marked and each is assigned a road number. As for the trails, most are well marked with identifying colored blazes and some, but not all, have a sign at the trail head specifying the name of the trail and what user groups are allowed on it.

At the date of this publication, there are no *specific* mountain biking policies for the Chattahoochee National Forest. The trails policy is: "Driving, riding, possessing, parking, or leaving any kind of transportation on a developed trail not designated, and so posted for that specific use" is prohibited. One can assume that mountain bikes fall under this policy and bikers are only welcome on trails signed for their use. Any unsigned, developed trail should be considered closed to bicycles. Bikes are allowed on gated and closed Forest Service roads, unless signed otherwise.

Currently all the trails and roads listed in this book are open to mountain bikes. It is possible that if excessive resource damage occurs or if visitor safety considerations arise, some trails may be closed. Just as possible is that more and more trails will be opened to bikers. It is very important that riders stay on open trails only and continue to use their best trail etiquette while in the forest. In this way the good image of bikers that exists in North Georgia will be maintained for years to come.

The outlook for increased riding possibilities on public lands is getting better and better in the South. The best way to see that this continues is to get involved by letting the proper authorities know of your wants and needs. Get to know the rangers and volunteer to help upgrade existing trails or build new ones. For further information contact:

Chattahoochee National Forest
USDA Forest Service
508 Oak Street, NW
Gainesville, GA 30501
706/536-0541

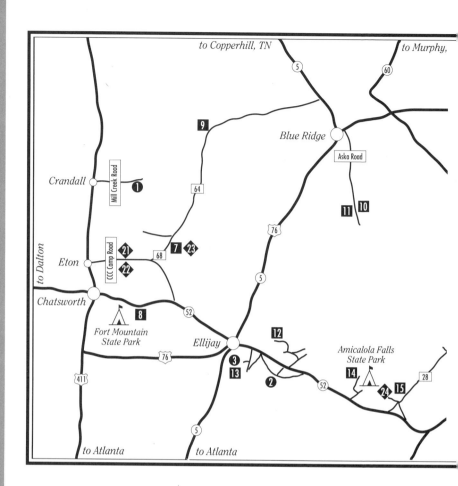

Blue Ridge

Aska Road

Crandall

Mill Creek Road

Eton

CCC Camp Road

to Dalton

Chatsworth

Fort Mountain
State Park

Ellijay

Amicalola Falls
State Park

to Atlanta

to Atlanta

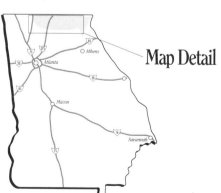

Athens

Atlanta

Macon

Savannah

Map Detail

Orientation Map

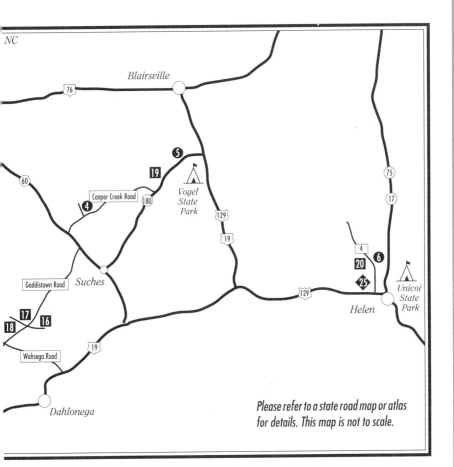

NC

Blairsville

76

Cooper Creek Road

5

19

4

180

Vogel State Park

60

129

19

Gaddistown Road Suches

Wahsega Road

17

18

16

19

Dahlonega

75

17

4

20

6

25

Unicoi State Park

129

Helen

Please refer to a state road map or atlas for details. This map is not to scale.

Easiest Trails

1– Rocky Flats
2– Blackberry Mountain
3– Red & White Loop
4– Cooper Creek
5– Sosebee Cove
6– Jasus Creek

More Difficult Trails

7– Bear Creek
8– Tatum Lead
9– South Fork
10– Lake Blue Ridge
11– Rich Mountain
12– Owltown

13– River Loop
14– Amicalola Falls
15– Bull Mountain
16– Canada Creek
17– Pleasant Valley
18– Winding Stairs
19– Duncan Ridge
20– Upper Hooch

Most Difficult Trails

21– Windy Gap
22– Milma
23– Mountaintown Creek
24– Nimblewill
25– Across the TN Divide

EASIEST TRAILS

Rocky Flats

An easy ride with relatively few hills and lots of views of the surrounding mountains. Be ready for one really fast downhill with numerous large whoop-te-doos near the end of the loop.

Start/Finish

From Crandall, GA , go east 4 miles on Mill Creek Rd. (FS 630), to second Rocky Flats ORV sign.

Trail Configuration

Loop

Surface

Single track • 4.7 miles
Gravel road • 1.1 miles

Highlights

ORV and ATV use, wildlife openings, timbercuts, whoop-te-doos, stream crossing

Total Distance

5.8 miles

Time Allowance

Beginner • 1 hour
Intermediate • 45 minutes
Advanced • 35 minutes

Mileposts

- **From start**– ride out ORV trail away from Mill Creek Road.
- **Mile 2.7**– road forks. Bear right on main road.
- **Mile 4.7**– steep downhill to stream crossing. Bear left up the hill after crossing the stream and then turn right on Mill Creek Road.
- **Mile 5.8**– finish.

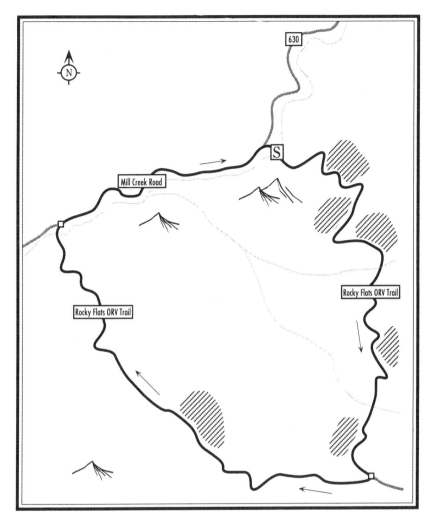

MAP KEY

Bike Route.........................	∿	Forest Service Rd. #.................	419
Other Trail or Road...........	∿	Road or Trail Name......	Rich Mountain Trail
Direction of Travel................	→	Foot Travel Only............	∿
Start/Finish..............................	S	Timber Cut or Clearing..	▨
Milepost.................................	□		
Public Land.......................	▭		
Other Land........................	▭		
Recreation Area...............	⛺		
Major Mountain........	⛰		
River, Lake, or Stream.....	∿		

Elevation Change

1120'   1560'   960'

②

Blackberry Mountain

This route can serve not only as a very pleasant ride on paved roads through the countryside, but also as a great warmup if you're competing in one of Mountaintown Outdoor Expeditions's many mountain bike races.

Start/Finish

Mountaintown Outdoor Expeditions. 4 miles from Elijay on GA 52, then right on Lower Cartecay Road.

Trail Configuration

Loop

Surface

Pavement • 5.8 miles

Highlights

Mountain views, apple orchards, farm land, exclusive community, Cartecay River, covered bridge

Total Distance

5.8 miles

Time Allowance

Beginner • 1 hour
Intermediate • 35 minutes
Advanced • 20 minutes

Mileposts

- **From start**– go east on Lower Cartecay Road.
- **Mile 1.3**– turn right on Old Clear Creek Road.
- **Mile 1.9**– the road forks twice. Bear right each time onto Blackberry Mountain Road
- **Mile 3.3**– after passing through a log cabin community, you'll see a wooden gate and fence. Go through gate, down drive and turn right on paved road.
- **Mile 4.1**– cross Cartecay River on covered bridge.
- **Mile 4.6**– turn right at the fork in the road.
- **Mile 5.2**– turn right at GA 52 to M.O.E.
- **Mile 5.8**– finish.

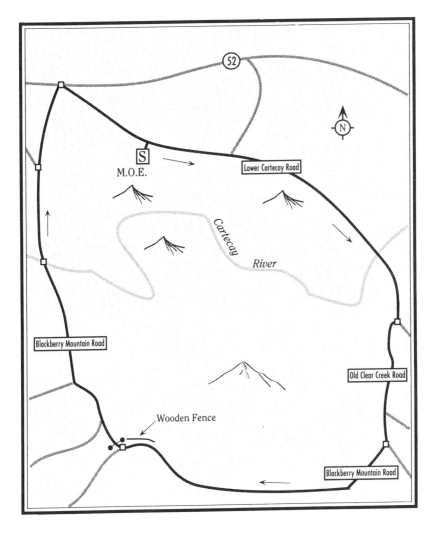

52

S
M.O.E.

Lower Cartecay Road

N

Cartecay

River

Blackberry Mountain Road

Old Clear Creek Road

Wooden Fence

Blackberry Mountain Road

MAP KEY

Bike Route.........................

Other Trail or Road...........

Direction of Travel................ →

Start/Finish.............................. S

Milepost................................ □

Public Land......................

Other Land......................

Recreation Area...............

Major Mountain........

River, Lake, or Stream.....

Forest Service Rd. #................ 419

Road or Trail Name...... Rich Mountain Trail

Foot Travel Only............

Timber Cut or Clearing..

1600'   1657'

1400'

Elevation Change

③ Red & White Loop

This short little loop is a great place for beginners to test their skills. You'll find short sections of tight single track, but mostly the going is pretty easy. This route can easily be added to the more difficult River Loop for an all-out ride. It gets its name from the alternating red and white blazes on the trees.

Start/Finish

From Mountaintown Outdoor Expeditions (directions on preceeding page), go back to GA 52 and take an immediate left onto the paved county road. Drive 0.5 miles to a Y-intersection. Turn right. Proceed 0.5 miles and turn left into Rich Mountain W.M.A. Cartecay Tract. Go 0.3 miles and park at gate.

Trail Configuration

Loop

Surface

Single track • 2.2 miles
Gravel road • 0.4 miles

Highlights

Hidden turns, short technical stretch, grassy roadbed, wildlife openings

Total Distance

2.6 miles

Time Allowance

Beginner • 45 minutes
Intermediate • 30 minutes
Advanced • 20 minutes

Alternate Start

Mountaintown Outdoor Expeditions

Mileposts

- **From start**– ride past gate out gravel road.
- **Mile 0.2**– small clearing just past gate on right. Turn right over the dirt barricade onto red & white blazed trail.
- **Mile 0.4**– trail splits. Turn right. Look for blazes.
- **Mile 1.2 - 1.4**– wildlife openings. Stay to right side and then continue to the right on the grassy roadbed.
- **Mile 2.4**– gate, turn left.
- **Mile 2.6**– finish.

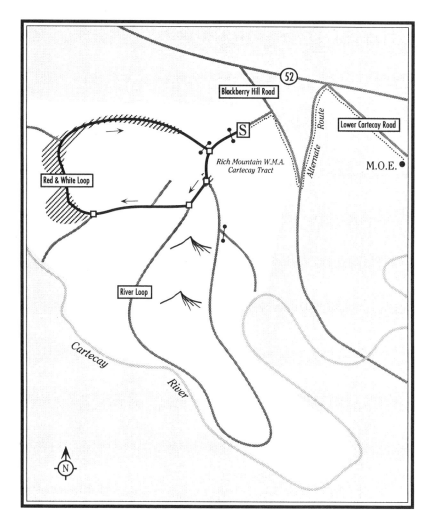

Labels on map:
- 52
- Blackberry Hill Road
- Lower Cartecay Road
- S
- Rich Mountain W.M.A. Cartecay Tract
- Alternate Route
- M.O.E.
- Red & White Loop
- River Loop
- Cartecay River
- N

MAP KEY

Bike Route.........................
Other Trail or Road...........
Direction of Travel................ →
Start/Finish.............................. S
Milepost.................................... □
Public Land.......................
Other Land........................
Recreation Area...............
Major Mountain........
River, Lake, or Stream.....

Forest Service Rd. #................ 419
Road or Trail Name...... Rich Mountain Trail
Foot Travel Only.............
Timber Cut or Clearing..

1600'
1400'

Elevation Change

Cooper Creek

As you circle Cooper Creek Scenic Area, you may begin to wonder if there is a hill around every bend. Fortunately none are too long and the wide gravel road gives you plenty of room to maneuver.

Start/Finish

Go 7.5 miles north of Suches on GA 60. Turn right on Cooper Creek Road. Start at the junction of the gravel FS 236.

Trail Configuration

Loop

Surface

Gravel road • 10.8 miles
Pavement • 1.6 miles

Highlights

Recreation area, scenic area, small cascades, views, rolling hills

Total Distance

12.4 miles

Time Allowance

Beginner • 2 hours
Intermediate • 1.5 hours
Advanced • 1 hour

Mileposts

- **From start**– ride towards the Recreation Area on FS 236
- **Mile 2.7**– just past the Recreation Area, turn right on FS 4.
- **Mile 3.5**– after passing the game checking station take the first right which is FS 39.
- **Mile 5.6**– turn right on FS 33A.
- **Mile 8.8**– just after crossing Cooper Creek, you'll climb a hill. Part way up, bear right onto FS 33.
- **Mile 10.8**– pavement begins.
- **Mile 12.4**– finish.

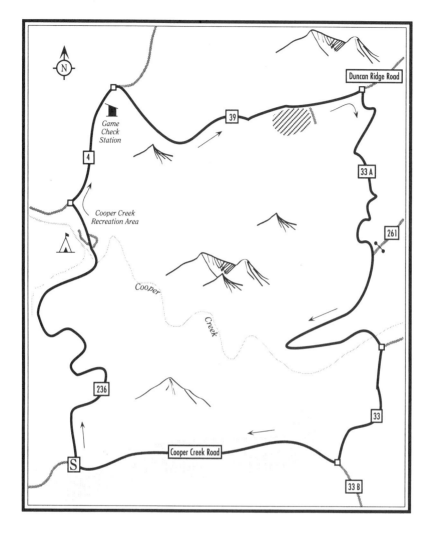

Duncan Ridge Road

39

33 A

261

Game
Check
Station

4

Cooper Creek
Recreation Area

Cooper

Creek

236

33

S

Cooper Creek Road

33 B

MAP KEY

Bike Route.........................

Other Trail or Road...........

Direction of Travel............... ⟶

Start/Finish............................ S

Milepost................................... □

Public Land......................

Other Land......................

Recreation Area............... ⛺

Major Mountain........

River, Lake, or Stream.....

Forest Service Rd. #................. 419

Road or Trail Name...... Rich Mountain Trail

Foot Travel Only............

Timber Cut or Clearing..

2240'   2840'
     2160'

Elevation Change

Sosebee Cove

A steep descent on the highway brings you to the mouth of the cove. Soon Slaughter Mountain looms ahead as you wind your way gradually back up, alongside Wolf Creek and through the length of the cove. The banked hairpin curves of GA 180 take you downhill back to your start at Vogel State Park.

Start/Finish

From Vogel State Park, drive 0.6 miles on GA 180 to a gravel pull off on the left. Start here.

Trail Configuration

Loop

Surface

Gravel road • 3.6 miles
Pavement • 4.2 miles

Highlights

Highway, Vogel State Park, small cascades and waterfalls, one steep uphill, steep paved downhills

Total Distance

7.8 miles

Time Allowance

Beginner • 2 hours
Intermediate • 1.25 hours
Advanced • 45 minutes

Mileposts

- **From start**– ride back to US 19/29 and turn left down hill.
- **Mile 2.3**– turn left on West Wolf Creek Road.
- **Mile 2.9**– Emory Road enters right. Grassy Knoll Road enters left. Continue straight over bridge onto gravel and then bear left at top of short hill. This is FS 107.
- **Mile 3.4**– road to Wolf Creek Wilderness School enters on left. Continue straight on FS 107.
- **Mile 6.0**– steep climb up to where FS 108 enters on the right. Stay on FS 107 by bearing to the left.
- **Mile 6.5**– turn left onto GA 180. It's all downhill from here.
- **Mile 7.8**– finish.

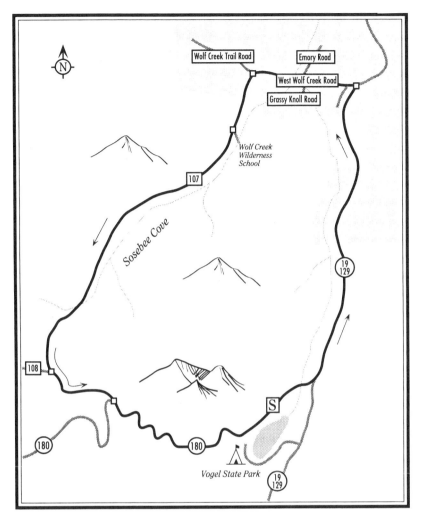

MAP KEY

Bike Route..........................

Other Trail or Road...........

Direction of Travel................ →

Start/Finish............................. S

Milepost.................................. □

Public Land......................

Other Land.......................

Recreation Area...............

Major Mountain........

River, Lake, or Stream.....

Forest Service Rd. #.................. 419

Road or Trail Name...... Rich Mountain Trail

Foot Travel Only............

Timber Cut or Clearing..

Elevation Change

Jasus Creek

Bears! This area is heavily populated with them. The warning sign at the beginning of the ride can make you jump at the slightest sound as you travel around this gated double track loop.

Start/Finish

From Helen, take GA 17/75 one mile north. Turn left on Alt. 75. Cross bridge and turn right. Follow this road 3 miles to the Chattahoochee W.M.A. Game Checking Station. Start here.

Trail Configuration

Loop w/ extension

Surface

Double track • 6.6 miles
Gravel road • 5.4 miles

Highlights

Bear territory, gated-off roadway, wildlife openings, small cascades, cool streams, spotty views

Total Distance

12 miles

Time Allowance

Beginner • 2.5 hours
Intermediate • 1.75 hours
Advanced • 1.25 hours

Mileposts

- **From start**– ride north on FS 44.
- **Mile 1.2**– turn right and cross Low Gap Creek over bridge. Stay on FS 44. (FS 44A continues straight.)
- **Mile 1.6**– FS 44C enters on left. Continue on FS 44.
- **Mile 3.7**– turn left past gate onto FS 44C.
- **Mile 10.3**– a series of whoop-te-doos brings you back to FS 44. Turn right.
- **Mile 10.7**– cross Low Gap Creek and bear left.
- **Mile 12.0**– finish.

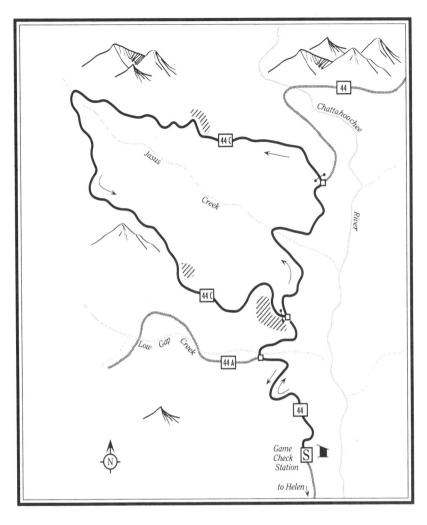

MAP KEY

Bike Route.........................
Other Trail or Road...........
Direction of Travel............... ⟶
Start/Finish............................ S
Milepost.................................... □
Public Land......................
Other Land.......................
Recreation Area............... Å
Major Mountain........
River, Lake, or Stream.....

Forest Service Rd. #................. 419
Road or Trail Name...... Rich Mountain Trail
Foot Travel Only.............
Timber Cut or Clearing..

2700'
1640'
Elevation Change

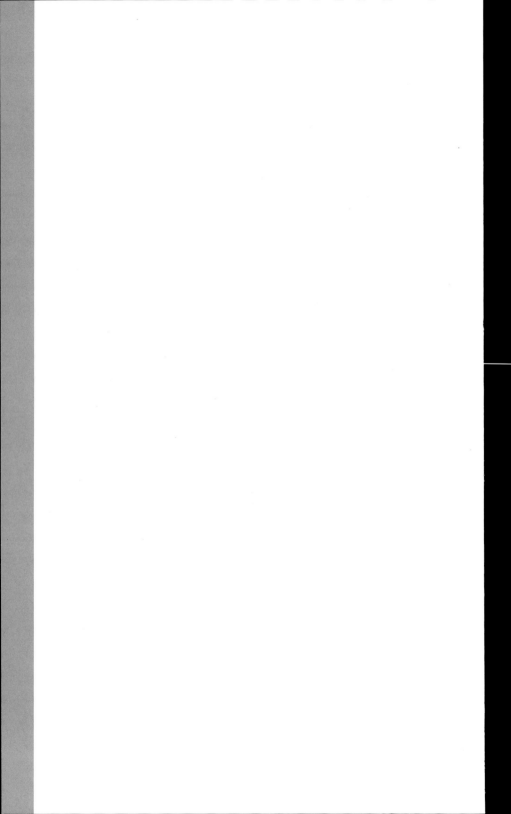

MORE DIFFICULT TRAILS

7– Bear Creek • 10.1 Miles
8– Tatum Lead • 14.5 Miles
9– South Fork • 8.1 Miles
10– Lake Blue Ridge • 7.5 Miles
11– Rich Mountain • 12.5 Miles
12– Owltown • 5.8 Miles
13– River Loop • 3.4 Miles
14– Amicalola Falls • 14.9 Miles
15– Bull Mountain • 14.6 Miles
16– Canada Creek • 14.8 Miles
17– Pleasant Valley • 24.3 Miles
18– Winding Stairs • 19.3 Miles
19– Duncan Ridge • 20.5 Miles
20– Upper Hooch • 15.4 Miles

Bear Creek

Starting and finishing at a beautiful waterfall, this trail has lots to offer. The single track is just technical enough to test your skills, while riding across and alongside the stream is very lovely.

Start/Finish

From Eton, go east from the stop light on CCC Camp Road 5.4 miles. The road name changes to FS 68. Continue another 9.1 miles to Barnes Creek Falls picnic area.

Trail Configuration

Loop

Surface

Single track • 9.2 miles
Gravel road • 0.9 miles

Highlights

Woods roads, whoop-te-doos, great views, stream crossings, The Bennett Poplar (huge old growth tree), one very steep uphill, waterfall, wildlife openings

Total Distance

10.1 miles

Time Allowance

Beginner • 2.25 hours
Intermediate • 1.5 hours
Advanced • 1.25 hours

Mileposts

- **From start–** ride uphill on FS 68.
- **Mile 0.4–** turn right through gate on Barnes Creek Road.
- **Mile 1.8–** turn right through gate on Bear Creek Trail.
- **Mile 2.1–** at wildlife opening, turn left over whoop-te-doo.
- **Mile 3.4–** Bear Creek Loop sign marks trail to left. Continue straight down the creek past Bennett Poplar.
- **Mile 4.4–** lower trailhead. Go 200 feet and trail continues on left side of road. Look for the blue blazes.
- **Mile 4.9–** turn left onto grassy roadbed.
- **Mile 5.3–** go left at road fork. Watch for blue blazed posts.
- **Mile 6.0–** Bear Creek Loop sign marks trail to left. Continue to the right.
- **Mile 8.3–** pass Bear Creek Trail sign on left. Stay straight.
- **Mile 9.6–** turn left on FS 68.
- **Mile 10.1–** finish.

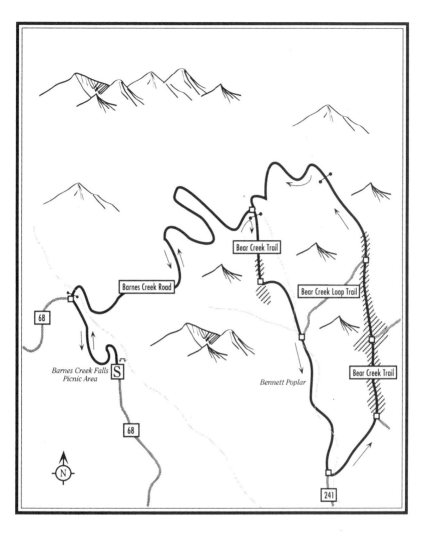

MAP KEY

Bike Route..........................

Other Trail or Road...........

Direction of Travel............... →

Start/Finish............................. S

Milepost................................... □

Public Land.......................

Other Land........................

Recreation Area............... ⛺

Major Mountain........

River, Lake, or Stream.....

Forest Service Rd. #................. 419

Road or Trail Name...... Rich Mountain Trail

Foot Travel Only............

Timber Cut or Clearing..

Elevation Change

2400'   2600'

1760'

8

Tatum Lead

A real teeth rattler at times, this route follows the ridgeline of Tatum Mountain out and back. The steep, whoop-te-doo filled side loop on the far end will definitely get your attention.

Start/Finish

From Chatsworth, go east on U.S. 52 for 11.3 miles. A gravel road on the right with a sign for Tatum Lead marks the start.

Trail Configuration

Out-and-back w/ loop extension

Surface

Single track • 7.3 miles
Gravel road • 7.2 miles

Highlights

Steep uphill and downhill, rocky trail, whoop-te-doos, spotty views, ATV and ORV use

Total Distance

14.5 miles

Time Allowance

Beginner • 3.5 hours
Intermediate • 2.5 hours
Advanced • 1.75 hours

Mileposts

- **From start**– ride south on Tatum Lead Road.
- **Mile 0.8**– you'll pass a gated road on the right and little further along another road on the left. Continue straight on at each junction.
- **Mile 0.9**– a road goes downhill to the right. Stay left.
- **Mile 1.8**– just past where a jeep road turns off to the right the road forks. Take the right fork.
- **Mile 5**– turn right on Rock Creek ATV Loop Trail.
- **Mile 6.4**– turn left (uphill) at ATV loop sign.
- **Mile 8.4**– turn left back onto Tatum Lead Road.
- **Mile 9.1**– pass turn off to Rock Creek ATV Loop Trail.
- **Mile 14.5**– finish.

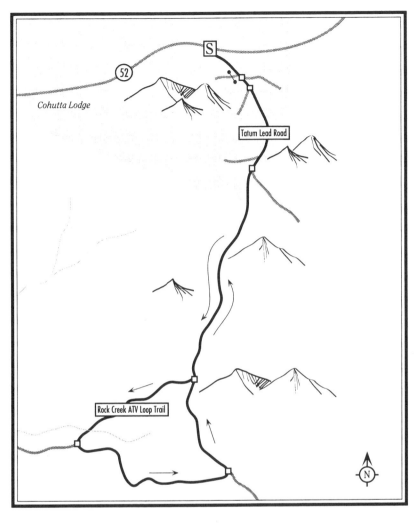

MAP KEY

Bike Route........................
Other Trail or Road...........
Direction of Travel.............. →
Start/Finish............................ $\boxed{S}$
Milepost................................. □
Public Land......................
Other Land......................
Recreation Area.............. ⛺
Major Mountain........
River, Lake, or Stream.....

Forest Service Rd. #................. $\boxed{419}$
Road or Trail Name...... $\boxed{\text{Rich Mountain Trail}}$
Foot Travel Only.............
Timber Cut or Clearing..

Elevation Change

9

South Fork

This is the only chance you get to ride alongside the Jacks River before it plunges into the Cohutta Wilderness. Wildlife openings make room for terrific views of the ridges above, and the return along the gravel road has some surprises of its own.

Start/Finish

From Eton, go east from the stop light on CCC Camp Road 5.4 miles. Here the name changes to FS 68. Continue another 11.3 miles to the jct. of FS 64 and turn right. Go 8.9 miles on FS 64 to Jacks River Fields. Start here.

Trail Configuration

Loop

Surface

Single track • 2.7 miles
Gravel road • 5.4 miles

Highlights

Stream crossings, lush, boggy areas, small mountain community, nice views

Total Distance

8.1 miles

Time Allowance

Beginner • 2 hours
Intermediate • 1.5 hours
Advanced • 1 hour

Warning: the gravel roads leading to the start are steep and curvy.

Mileposts

- **From start**– go right out of campground, cross river and turn left onto South Fork Trail.
- **Mile 0.6**– Benton Mackaye Trail enters from right.
- **Mile 2.2**– Benton Mackaye Trail exits to right. Stay left.
- **Mile 2.7**– cross dirt barricade onto woods road.
- **Mile 2.9**– ford river, ride up short hill and turn right on FS 126.
- **Mile 3.6**– Jones Settlement. Continue straight on FS 126.
- **Mile 4.2**– turn right on FS 64.
- **Mile 7.4**– Dyer Gap. 64A exits to left. Stay right on FS 64.
- **Mile 8.1**– finish.

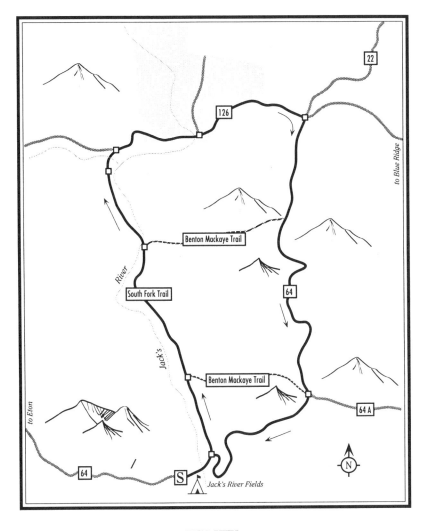

MAP KEY

Bike Route.........................	〜	Forest Service Rd. #.................	419
Other Trail or Road...........	〜	Road or Trail Name......	Rich Mountain Trail
Direction of Travel................	→	Foot Travel Only.............	〜
Start/Finish............................	S	Timber Cut or Clearing..	▨
Milepost..................................	□		
Public Land......................	▭		
Other Land.......................	▭		
Recreation Area...............	⛺		
Major Mountain........	⛰		
River, Lake, or Stream.....	〜		

Elevation Change

Lake Blue Ridge

Taking advantage of the shorter half of the Rich Mountain Trail, this route winds its way down and alongside Lake Blue Ridge on terrific single track. Be prepared for a long climb at the end.

Start/Finish

From Blue Ridge, take Old U.S. 76 east to the edge of town. Turn right on Aska Road and drive 5 miles to Deep Gap. Trailhead parking is just over the top of hill.

Trail Configuration

Loop

Surface

Single track • 3.4 miles
Gravel road • 2.2 miles
Pavement • 1.9 miles

Highlights

Long downhill on single track, well marked, lake views, vacation homes, uphill to finish

Total Distance

7.5 miles

Time Allowance

Beginner • 2 hours
Intermediate • 1.5 hours
Advanced • 1 hour

Mileposts

- **From start**– cross Aska Road onto Rich Mountain Trail (marked with white blazes).
- **Mile 2.2**– old roadbed enters from right. Bear left.
- **Mile 2.3**– take a sharp right off old roadbed and cross small stream. Lake Blue Ridge will be to your right.
- **Mile 3.4**– Rich Mountain Trail trailhead. 5-way interchange. Bear right on second gravel road to the right.
- **Mile 4.7**– turn left at T-intersection.
- **Mile 4.9**– turn right on Campbell Camp Road.
- **Mile 5.6**– turn left on Aska Road.
- **Mile 7.5**– finish.

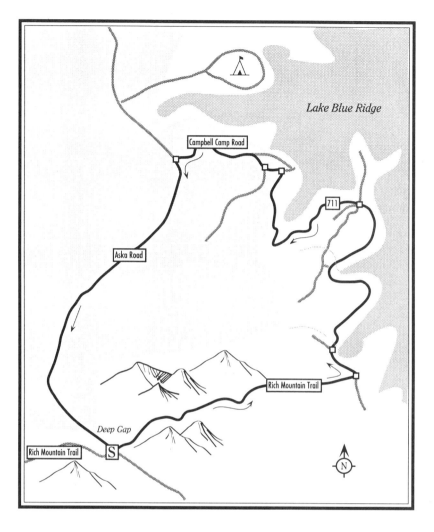

Lake Blue Ridge

Campbell Camp Road

711

Aska Road

Rich Mountain Trail

Deep Gap

Rich Mountain Trail

S

N

MAP KEY

Bike Route..........................	Forest Service Rd. #.................. 419
Other Trail or Road...........	Road or Trail Name...... Rich Mountain Trail
Direction of Travel............... →	Foot Travel Only............
Start/Finish............................ S	Timber Cut or Clearing..
Milepost.................................. □	
Public Land......................	
Other Land.......................	
Recreation Area..............	
Major Mountain........	
River, Lake, or Stream.....	

2520'   2120'
1680'

Elevation Change

11

Rich Mountain

Fabulous single track makes this one of Georgia's most famous bike trails! On this route, a paved downhill takes you to the Toccoa River before going up, up, up to the trail. You then ride over the top of the mountain on the ridge.

Start/Finish

From Blue Ridge, take Old U.S. 76 east to the edge of town. Turn right on Aska Road and drive 5 miles to Deep Gap. Trailhead parking is just over top of hill.

Trail Configuration

Loop

Surface

Single track • 4.9 miles
Gravel road • 3.9 miles
Pavement • 3.7 miles

Highlights

Views, long rocky downhill, river rapids, vacation homes, small stream crossings

Total Distance

12.5 miles

Time Allowance

Beginner • 3 hours
Intermediate • 2.25 hours
Advanced • 1.5 hours

Mileposts

- **From start**– turn right from trailhead parking area, downhill on Aska Road
- **Mile 3.7**– turn right onto gravel road #509. It's marked by a sign for Rich Mountain W.M.A.
- **Mile 6.7**– Benton Mackaye Trail exits right.
- **Mile 7.6**– Stanley Gap. Turn right on Rich Mountain Trail. The entrance is somewhat hidden. Look for two dirt barricades and tire tracks. The trail sign is just past the barricades about 50 feet off the road (white square blazes).
- **Mile 8.2**– Benton Mackaye Trail enters right.
- **Mile 10.1**– Benton Mackaye Trail exits left.
- **Mile 12.5**– finish.

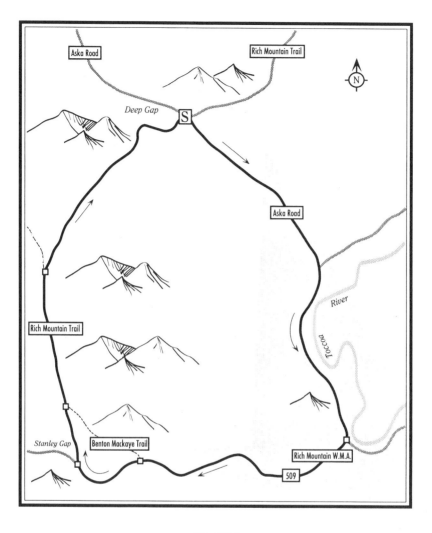

MAP KEY

Bike Route........................
Other Trail or Road...........
Direction of Travel............... →
Start/Finish............................ S
Milepost.................................. □
Public Land......................
Other Land.......................
Recreation Area...............
Major Mountain........
River, Lake, or Stream.....

Forest Service Rd. #................. 419
Road or Trail Name...... Rich Mountain Trail
Foot Travel Only............
Timber Cut or Clearing..

Elevation Change

3442'
2120'
1720'

Owltown

Rolling hills and a steep climb take you to the top of Owltown Mountain. After brake-screeching your way to the bottom, you'll follow along and crisscross Owltown Creek.

Start/Finish

From GA 5 in Ellijay, go 4.8 miles to Big Creek Road. Turn left. Go 0.3 miles. Turn left and go 0.7 miles towards Mt. Zion Baptist Church. Turn left at stop sign. Go 0.1 miles and turn right. Go 2.2 miles. Park at pulloff on right just before fording Owltown Creek. The trail start is hidden behind a dirt barricade on the right.

Trail Configuration

Loop

Surface

Single track • 4.9 miles
Gravel road • 0.9 miles

Highlights

Rolling single track, steep hills, wildlife openings, stream crossings, spotty views, ATV use

Total Distance

5.8 miles

Time Allowance

Beginner • 2 hours
Intermediate • 1.25 hours
Advanced • 45 minutes

Alternate Start

Mountaintown Outdoor Expeditions

Mileposts

- **From start**– ride over dirt barricade onto trail.
- **Mile 0.3**– trail splits. Go left following orange blazes.
- **Mile 1.0**– roadbed to right. Follow orange blaze to left.
- **Mile 1.1**– roadbed to right. Follow orange blaze to left.
- **Mile 1.3**– roads junction. Turn right uphill. Look for orange blazes.
- **Mile 2.9**– after steep climb and even steeper descent you come to an old dirt road. Bear right on road up slight hill.
- **Mile 3.1**– turn sharply to right down the hill.
- **Mile 4.0**– cross stream and turn right (orange blazes).
- **Mile 4.9**– gravel road. Turn right.
- **Mile 5.8**– finish.

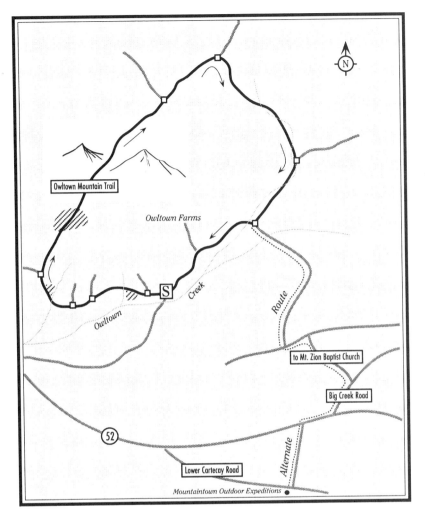

MAP KEY

Bike Route........................
Other Trail or Road...........
Direction of Travel............... →
Start/Finish............................ S
Milepost.................................... □
Public Land........................
Other Land........................
Recreation Area............... ⚐
Major Mountain........
River, Lake, or Stream.....

Forest Service Rd. #................. 419
Road or Trail Name...... Rich Mountain Trail
Foot Travel Only.............
Timber Cut or Clearing..

2171'
1400'

Elevation Change

13

River Loop

This technical route alongside the Cartecay River is a must. It's a short ride that packs a lot of punch. If it's warm, give yourself time for a swim at one of the sandy beaches below the rapids.

Start/Finish

Take GA 52 east from Elijay 3.5 miles. Here Lower Cartecay Road on the right takes you to Mountaintown Outdoor Expeditions. Instead, turn even sharper right onto the unmarked county road. Go 0.5 miles and turn back to right. Go 0.5 miles to the sign for Rich Mountain W.M.A. Cartecay Tract. Turn left on gravel road and go 0.3 miles to gate. Park and start here.

Trail Configuration

Loop

Surface

Single track • 2.3 miles
Gravel road • 1.1 miles

Highlights

Great single track, one extremely steep downhill, Cartecay River, rapids, beaches, boggy areas, technical riding

Total Distance

3.4 miles

Time Allowance

Beginner • 1 hour
Intermediate • 45 minutes
Advanced • 30 minutes

Alternate Start

Mountaintown Outdoor Expeditions

Mileposts

- **From start**– ride past gate out gravel road.
- **Mile 0.1**– gated road enters right, stay to left.
- **Mile 0.2**– small clearing with hidden trail entering on right. Continue to left on road.
- **Mile 0.7**– turn-around area with gated road entering on left. Continue straight across turn-around onto trail.
- **Mile 1.2**– steep downhill to river.
- **Mile 3.0**– Red & White Loop Trail enters from left. Stay straight.
- **Mile 3.1**– Cross dirt barricade and bear left onto road.
- **Mile 3.4**– finish.

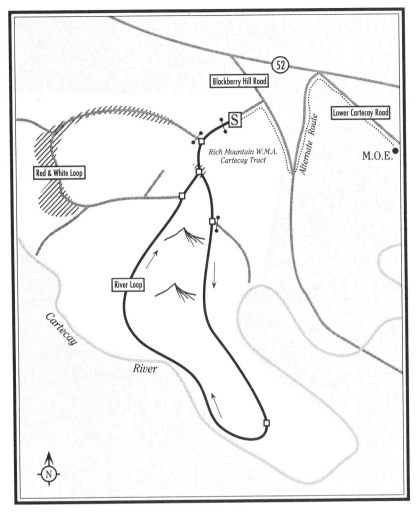

52

Blackberry Hill Road

S

Lower Cartecay Road

Rich Mountain W.M.A.
Cartecay Tract

Alternate Route

M.O.E.

Red & White Loop

River Loop

Cartecay

River

N

MAP KEY

Bike Route..........................

Other Trail or Road...........

Direction of Travel................ →

Start/Finish.............................. S

Milepost.................................... □

Public Land.....................

Other Land.......................

Recreation Area...............

Major Mountain........

River, Lake, or Stream.....

Forest Service Rd. #................. 419

Road or Trail Name...... Rich Mountain Trail

Foot Travel Only.............

Timber Cut or Clearing..

1600'   1648'

1360'

Elevation Change

14

Amicalola Falls

This is a superb ride. Starting with a top-of-Georgia view, you'll do a little climbing, then a hidden ATV trail takes you into a beautiful valley. You're not there long before making an arduous climb over Frosty Mountain and back to the falls.

Start/Finish

Amicalola Falls State Park. Top of falls parking lot.

Trail Configuration

Loop w/ extension

Surface

Single track • 5.6 miles
Gravel road • 8.7 miles
Pavement • 0.6 miles

Highlights

Waterfall view, stream crossings, ATV & ORV use, very rocky, mountain farms

Total Distance

14.9 miles

Time Allowance

Beginner • 4.5 hours
Intermediate • 3 hours
Advanced • 2 hours

Mileposts

- **From start–** ride uphill on road across from parking lot.
- **Mile 0.1–** turn right at first paved road.
- **Mile 1.6–** Nimblewill Gap road exits right. Stay to left on High Shoals Road.
- **Mile 2.1–** High Shoals Baptist Church. Stay straight.
- **Mile 2.7–** ford two streams and then turn right on ATV/ORV trail. It is marked with a sign.
- **Mile 4.7–** turn right on FS 357.
- **Mile 6.7–** turn right on FS 28.
- **Mile 10.1–** Nimblewill Gap. Turn right on Nimblewill Gap Road.
- **Mile 11.1–** road forks. Bear left.
- **Mile 13.3–** turn left on High Shoals Road.
- **Mile 14.9–** finish.

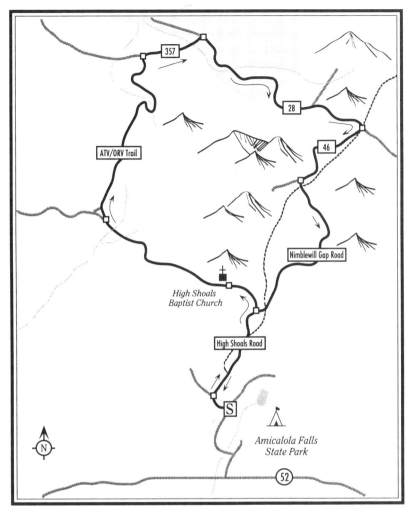

Labels on map:

357

28

46

ATV/ORV Trail

Nimblewill Gap Road

High Shoals
Baptist Church

High Shoals Road

S

Amicalola Falls
State Park

52

N

MAP KEY

Bike Route........................ ∿

Other Trail or Road........... ∿

Direction of Travel................ ⟶

Start/Finish............................ S

Milepost............................. □

Public Land......................

Other Land......................

Recreation Area............... ⛺

Major Mountain........

River, Lake, or Stream.....

Forest Service Rd. #................. 419

Road or Trail Name...... Rich Mountain Trail

Foot Travel Only.............

Timber Cut or Clearing..

2554'   3200'

2000'

Elevation Change

15

Bull Mountain

As you climb the forest roads, you'll find they get narrower and narrower until at last you're on pure single track. Watch out for the surprisingly fast downhills over the numerous whoop-te-doos or they may send you flying.

Start/Finish

From Amicalola Falls State Park, drive east on GA 52 for 6.8 miles. Turn left at sign for Nimblewill Baptist Church. Go 1 mile. Park and start at church.

Trail Configuration

Loop

Surface

Single track • 6.4 miles
Gravel road • 8.2 miles

Highlights

Timber cuts, loose gravel, spotty views, stream crossings, steep rocky uphill, whoop-te-doos

Total Distance

14.6 miles

Time Allowance

Beginner • 2.5 hours
Intermediate • 1.75 hours
Advanced • 1.25 hours

Mileposts

- **From start**– ride towards game checking station on FS 28.
- **Mile 0.4**– gated FS 83 enters left. Stay on FS 28.
- **Mile 2.1**– turn left on FS 77 up past game check station.
- **Mile 3.5**– turn left on FS 77A.
- **Mile 5.3**– FS 877 enters on right. Stay straight on FS 77A.
- **Mile 5.4**– after a steep climb the road forks. The left fork fords the stream. Take the right fork through the gate.
- **Mile 5.6**– closed road exits right. Stay to left by stream.
- **Mile 7.8**– ford stream and take immediate left turn up steep rocky grade and under gate.
- **Mile 11.1**– trail forks. Take the right fork down hill.
- **Mile 12.0**– turn right on FS 83.
- **Mile 14.2**– turn right on FS 28.
- **Mile 14.6**– finish.

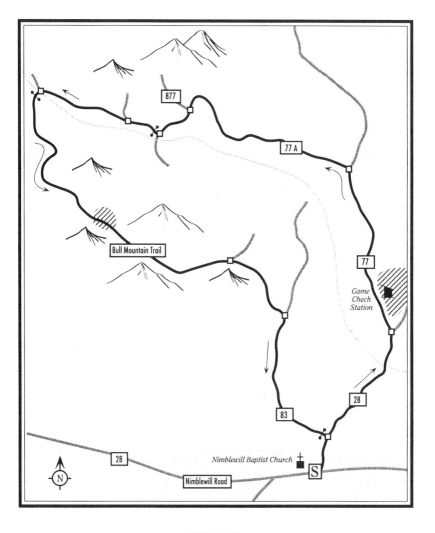

MAP KEY

Bike Route.........................		Forest Service Rd. #..................	419
Other Trail or Road...........		Road or Trail Name......	Rich Mountain Trail
Direction of Travel...............	→	Foot Travel Only.............	
Start/Finish...........................	S	Timber Cut or Clearing..	
Milepost..................................	□		
Public Land.......................			
Other Land........................			
Recreation Area...............	Λ		
Major Mountain........			
River, Lake, or Stream.....			

Elevation Change

16

Canada Creek

It seems as if this ride is constantly going downhill while you work your way from where the Appalachian Trail crosses the high ridges. You'll find a hidden single track surprise as you traverse Canada Creek Road over to Pleasant Valley and back up to the start.

Start/Finish

From Dahlonega go 2.2 miles north on GA 60. Turn left on Wahsega Road. Go 8.5 miles and turn right on FS 80 at Camp Frank Merril. Go 2.8 miles to Cooper Gap. Start here.

Trail Configuration

Loop

Surface

Single track • 0.8 miles
Gravel road • 11.4 miles
Pavement • 2.6 miles

Highlights

Great views, lots of downhill, old farm houses, old bridge, streams, loose gravel

Total Distance

14.8 miles

Time Allowance

Beginner • 3 hours
Intermediate • 2 hours
Advanced • 1.25 hours

Mileposts

- **From start**– ride east on FS 42 towards Suches.
- **Mile 6.6**– gravel road changes to paved road.
- **Mile 7.0**– turn left on gravel Canada Creek Road. It looks like a driveway. Continue up past houses.
- **Mile 7.6**– road forks. Bear right.
- **Mile 9.3**– road closed barricade and an old wooden bridge. Cross bridge and go over dirt barricades up grassy roadbed.
- **Mile 10.1**– dirt barricade and gated road to right. Bear left.
- **Mile 10.4**– road enters from left. Bear right past houses.
- **Mile 11.3**– turn left onto paved road.
- **Mile 14.8**– finish.

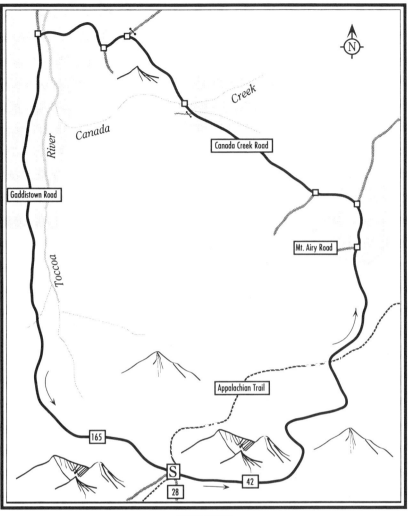

MAP KEY

Bike Route..........................
Other Trail or Road...........
Direction of Travel............... →
Start/Finish............................ S
Milepost.................................... □
Public Land........................
Other Land.........................
Recreation Area............... ⚐
Major Mountain........
River, Lake, or Stream.....

Forest Service Rd. #.................. 419
Road or Trail Name...... Rich Mountain Trail
Foot Travel Only.............
Timber Cut or Clearing..

2820'   2991'

2120'

Elevation Change

17

Pleasant Valley

A quick descent drops you into beautiful valley farmland, surrounded by mountains. Here you roll alongside the Toccoa River. Just as you start the long climb back to the high ridges, you'll pass a fish hatchery with thousands of young trout.

Start/Finish

From Dahlonega go 2.2 miles north on GA 60. Turn left on Wahsega Road. Go 8.5 miles and turn right on FS 80 at Camp Frank Merril. Go 2.8 miles to Cooper Gap. Start here.

Trail Configuration

Loop

Surface

Gravel road • 13.4 miles
Pavement • 10.9 miles

Highlights

Valley farms, Toccoa River, highway, Chattahoochee National Fish Hatchery, rocky road, mountain views from above and below, quiet streams

Total Distance

24.3 miles

Time Allowance

Beginner • 4 hours
Intermediate • 3 hours
Advanced • 2 hours

Mileposts

- **From start–** ride north (downhill) on FS 165.
- **Mile 4.8–** just before crossing Toccoa River, turn left on Northside Road.
- **Mile 6.2–** turn right on Parker Road, cross river and turn left on GA 60.
- **Mile 11.7–** turn left on gravel Fish Hatchery Road (FS 69). Stay on this road for the next 8.9 miles.
- **Mile 16.5–** Chattahoochee National Fish Hatchery.
- **Mile 20.1–** road forks. FS 69A enters right. Bear left up the hill and stay on FS 69.
- **Mile 20.6–** Hightower Gap. Turn left on FS 42.
- **Mile 24.3–** finish.

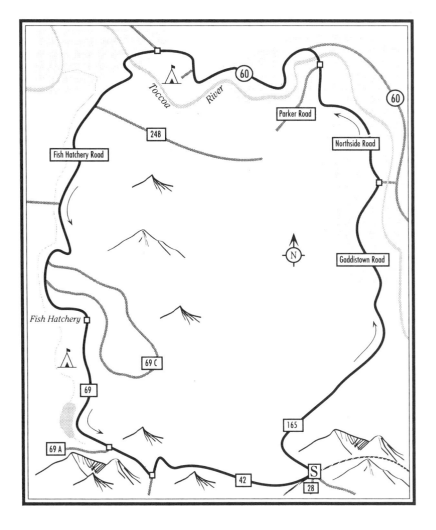

MAP KEY

Bike Route.........................	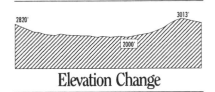	Forest Service Rd. #.................	419
Other Trail or Road...........		Road or Trail Name......	Rich Mountain Trail
Direction of Travel................	→	Foot Travel Only............	
Start/Finish..........................	S	Timber Cut or Clearing..	
Milepost.................................	□		
Public Land......................			
Other Land......................			
Recreation Area...............	⋏		
Major Mountain........			
River, Lake, or Stream.....			

Elevation Change

2820'   3013'   2000'

18

Winding Stairs

This is forest road ridge riding at its best. You parallel the Appalachian Trail the first 7.5 miles along some of Georgia's highest peaks before dropping quickly to the valley below. Lookout for U.S. Army Rangers, as you'll pass their camp just before the steep climb back to the start.

Start/Finish

From Dahlonega go 2.2 miles north on GA 60. Turn left on Wahsega Road. Go 8.5 miles and turn right on FS 80 at Camp Frank Merril. Go 2.8 miles to Cooper Gap. Start here.

Trail Configuration

Loop

Surface

Gravel road • 19.3 miles

Highlights

Ridge riding, views, long steep downhill, game checking station, 4-H Camp, U.S. Army Ranger Camp, rocky roadbed

Total Distance

19.3 miles

Time Allowance

Beginner • 4.5 hours
Intermediate • 3.25 hours
Advanced • 2 hours

Mileposts

- **From start**– ride west along ridgeline on FS 42.
- **Mile 3.6**– Hightower Gap. FS 69 enters right. Stay on FS 42.
- **Mile 4.9**– FS 42A enters right. Stay on FS 42.
- **Mile 7.4**– Winding Stairs Gap. Intersection of FS 42, 77, and 58. Turn left, downhill on FS 77.
- **Mile 11.0**– FS 77A exits to right. Bear left and stay on FS 77.
- **Mile 12.3**– just past game check station, turn left on FS 28.
- **Mile 14.8**– roads jct. at mail boxes. Stay straight on FS 28.
- **Mile 15.5**– 4-H Camp Wahsega on right.
- **Mile 16.5**– U.S. Army Ranger Camp Frank Merril on left. Cross 100 yds. of pavement and continue uphill on FS 80.
- **Mile 19.3**– finish.

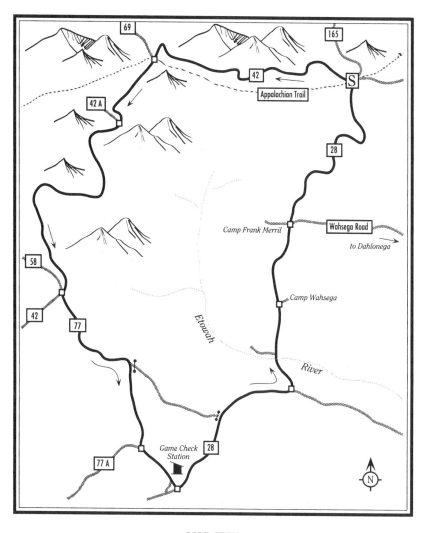

MAP KEY

Bike Route.......................... ∿

Other Trail or Road........... ∿

Direction of Travel............... →

Start/Finish............................ ⒮

Milepost.................................. □

Public Land......................

Other Land........................

Recreation Area............... ⛺

Major Mountain........ 🏔

River, Lake, or Stream.....

Forest Service Rd. #................. 419

Road or Trail Name...... Rich Mountain Trail

Foot Travel Only.............

Timber Cut or Clearing..

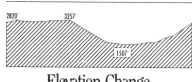

Elevation Change

19

Duncan Ridge

Starting with a fast downhill to Lake Winfield Scott, this ride goes down, down, down for close to 10 miles before a steady climb up onto Duncan Ridge. It's then a ridgeline ride back to the start.

Start/Finish

From Vogel State Park, go 3.5 miles on GA 180 to its jct. with Duncan Ridge Road. Start here.

Trail Configuration

Loop

Surface

Gravel road • 16.3 miles
Pavement • 4.2 miles

Highlights

Long, fast, swooping downhill on pavement, rocky roads, views

Total Distance

20.5 miles

Time Allowance

Beginner • 3 hours
Intermediate • 2.5 hours
Advanced • 1.75 hour

Mileposts

- **From start**– ride west (downhill) on GA 180.
- **Mile 2.7**– Lake Winfield Scott on left.
- **Mile 3.3**– turn right on Cooper Creek Road. 0.3 miles down the road will be a sign for Cooper Creek W.M.A.
- **Mile 4.2**– pavement ends and gravel FS 33 begins. Stay on this road for the next 5.6 miles.
- **Mile 9.8**– bear right onto FS 33A. Go down hill and cross Cooper Creek on a bridge.
- **Mile 11.6**– FS 261 exits right. Stay on FS 33A.
- **Mile 13.0**– junction FS 39. Turn right.
- **Mile 13.4**– unmarked road exits right. Stay left on FS 39 and continue to climb up the ridge.
- **Mile 20.5**– finish.

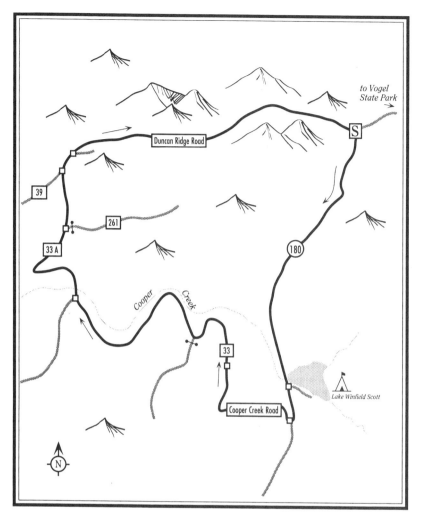

to Vogel
State Park

Duncan Ridge Road

39

261

33 A

Cooper Creek

180

33

Cooper Creek Road

Lake Winfield Scott

N

MAP KEY

Bike Route..........................

Other Trail or Road...........

Direction of Travel............... →

Start/Finish............................. S

Milepost.................................. □

Public Land.......................

Other Land.......................

Recreation Area...............

Major Mountain........

River, Lake, or Stream.....

Forest Service Rd. #................. 419

Road or Trail Name...... Rich Mountain Trail

Foot Travel Only.............

Timber Cut or Clearing..

3280'   3750'

2360'

Elevation Change

20

Upper Hooch

Be prepared to ride this with wet feet, as you start by fording the Chattahoochee River. You'll climb steadily with some steep pitches on a gated roadbed for the first 6 miles before returning alongside the river on the gravel Chattahoochee River Road.

Start/Finish

From Helen drive 1 mile north on GA 17/75. Turn left on Alt. 75. Cross river and turn right. Go 2.9 miles to W.M.A. Chattahoochee Game Check Station.

Trail Configuration

Loop

Surface

Gravel road • 15.4 miles

Highlights

Chattahoochee River, small waterfalls, great views, timber cuts, wildlife openings, river ford

Total Distance

15.4 miles

Time Allowance

Beginner • 3 hours
Intermediate • 2.25 hours
Advanced • 1.5 hours

Mileposts

- **From start**– ride south on FS 44 back towards Helen.
- **Mile 0.7**– turn left on FS 178 and ford river.
- **Mile 1.7**– a gated road enters from the right.
- **Mile 2.8**– gate across road. Continue around it.
- **Mile 6.0**– gate across road. Continue around it, then turn left on FS 44.
- **Mile 8.8**– FS 44F enters from right. Bear left alongside river.
- **Mile 10.1**– FS 44E and 44D enter from right.
- **Mile 11.7**– FS 44C enters from right.
- **Mile 13.7**– the other end of FS 44C enters on right.
- **Mile 14.0**– cross Low Gap Creek and bear left. FS 44A enters on right.
- **Mile 15.4**– finish.

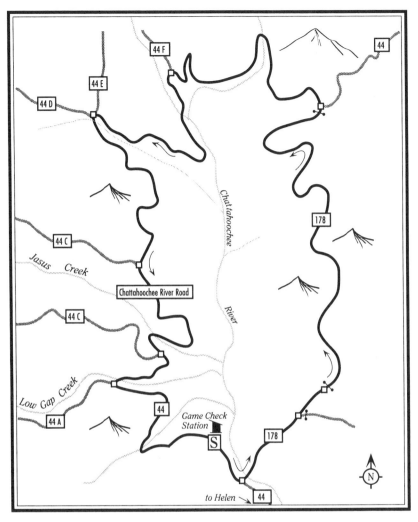

MAP KEY

Bike Route........................	Forest Service Rd. #................. 419
Other Trail or Road...........	Road or Trail Name...... Rich Mountain Trail
Direction of Travel............... →	Foot Travel Only............
Start/Finish............................ S	Timber Cut or Clearing..
Milepost.................................... □	
Public Land......................	
Other Land......................	
Recreation Area.............. △	
Major Mountain........	
River, Lake, or Stream.....	

Elevation Change

2920'
1640'
1560'

MOST DIFFICULT TRAILS

21

Windy Gap

A long climb up an ORV trail takes you to Lake Conasauga, a high lake surrounded by mountains. Hold on to your socks! The descent is steep, rocky, difficult, and a real blast.

Start/Finish

From the stoplight in Eton, go east on CCC Camp Road 4.3 miles to the Cohutta District Work Center. Start here.

Trail Configuration

Loop

Surface

Single track • 4 miles
Gravel road • 6.6 miles
Pavement • 1.9 miles

Highlights

Views, ORV and ATV use,long steep climb, Lake Conasauga, very technical downhill single track, banked turns

Total Distance

12.5 miles

Time Allowance

Beginner • 4 hours
Intermediate • 3 hours
Advanced • 2 hours

Mileposts

- **From start**– ride east on CCC Camp Road.
- **Mile 1.9**– pavement turns to gravel. Turn left on FS 78.
- **Mile 2.7**– gate across road. Go around it.
- **Mile 3.0**– road forks. Stay to left on FS 78.
- **Mile 4.6**– gated woods roads enters from right.
- **Mile 4.7**– turn right up Tibbs ORV Trail.
- **Mile 5.3**– gate across road. Continue around it.
- **Mile 6.1**– upper trailhead for Tibbs ORV Trail. Turn left on FS 68.
- **Mile 6.2**– road forks. The right fork goes to Lake Conasauga. Take the left fork to continue the route.
- **Mile 6.9**– turn left on Windy Gap Cycle Trail.
- **Mile 9.2**– Milma Creek ATV trail enters from left.
- **Mile 10.9**– turn left onto gravel road FS 218.
- **Mile 12.5**– finish.

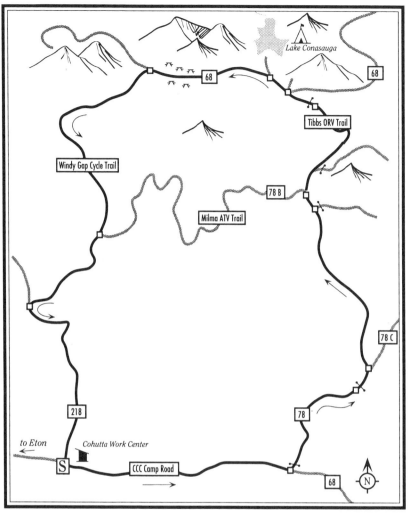

Lake Conasauga

68

68

Tibbs ORV Trail

Windy Gap Cycle Trail

78 B

Milma ATV Trail

78 C

218

78

to Eton

Cohutta Work Center

S

CCC Camp Road

68

N

MAP KEY

Bike Route.........................	
Other Trail or Road...........	
Direction of Travel.............. →	
Start/Finish............................	$\boxed{S}$
Milepost................................... □	
Public Land.....................	
Other Land.......................	
Recreation Area..............	
Major Mountain........	
River, Lake, or Stream.....	

Forest Service Rd. #................	419
Road or Trail Name......	Rich Mountain Trail
Foot Travel Only.............	
Timber Cut or Clearing..	

3263'

880'
860'

Elevation Change

22

Milma

Used by both ATV's and ORV's, this route climbs steeply up gravel roads before taking to the side of Grassy Mountain on the technical Milma Creek Trail. Fast, banked turns and whoop-te-doos bring you back to the start.

Start/Finish

From the stoplight in Eton, go east on CCC Camp Road 4.3 miles to the Cohutta District Work Center. Start here.

Trail Configuration

Loop

Surface

Single track • 2.9 miles
Gravel road • 7.2 miles
Pavement • 1.9 miles

Highlights

Views of Fort Mountain, timber cuts, ORV and ATV use, wildlife openings

Total Distance

12 miles

Time Allowance

Beginner • 2.5 hours
Intermediate • 1.75 hours
Advanced • 1.25 hours

Mileposts

- **From start**– ride east on CCC Camp Road.
- **Mile 1.9**– pavement turns to gravel. Turn left on FS 78.
- **Mile 2.7**– gate across road. Continue around.
- **Mile 3.0**– road forks. Continue left on FS 78.
- **Mile 4.6**– gated woods road to right.
- **Mile 4.7**– turn left on FS 78B. This is the Milma Creek ATV Trail.
- **Mile 8.5**– junction Windy Gap Cycle Trail. Turn left.
- **Mile 10.2**– turn left on gravel road FS 218.
- **Mile 12.0**– finish.

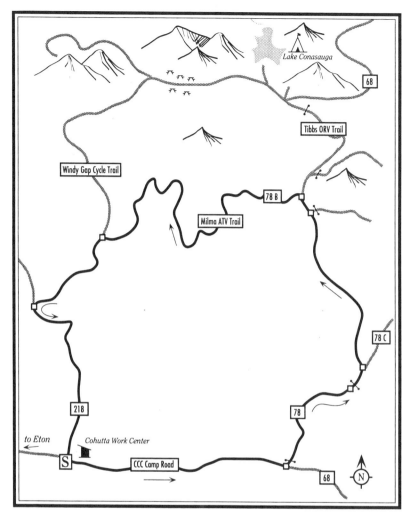

Lake Conasauga

68

Tibbs ORV Trail

Windy Gap Cycle Trail

78 B

Milma ATV Trail

78 C

218

78

to Eton

Cohutta Work Center

78

S

CCC Camp Road

68

N

MAP KEY

Bike Route.........................

Other Trail or Road...........

Direction of Travel...............   →

Start/Finish.............................   S

Milepost....................................   □

Public Land.......................

Other Land.......................

Recreation Area...............   Λ̈

Major Mountain........

River, Lake, or Stream.....

Forest Service Rd. #.................   419

Road or Trail Name......   Rich Mountain Trail

Foot Travel Only.............

Timber Cut or Clearing..

1906'
880'
860'

Elevation Change

23

Mountaintown Creek

This is one of the most remote rides in North Georgia. You'll climb to the ridgeline bordering the Cohutta Wilderness before dropping down into the Mountaintown Creek Gorge with its many cascades and waterfalls. It's then a short ride through the valley before the climb back to Barnes Creek Falls.

Start/Finish

From the stoplight in Eton, go east on CCC Camp Road for 6.2 miles. Here the road turns to gravel and becomes FS 68. Continue another 9.1 miles to Barnes Creek Falls Picnic Area. Start here.

Trail Configuration
Loop

Surface
Single track • 5.4 miles
Gravel road • 13.6 miles
Pavement • 0.6 miles

Highlights
Remote, views, cascades and waterfalls, multiple stream crossings, boggy areas, long climb, mountain farms

Total Distance
19.6 miles

Time Allowance
Beginner • 5 hours
Intermediate • 3.25 hours
Advanced • 2.5 hours

Mileposts

- **From start**– ride uphill on FS 68.
- **Mile 2.2**– turn right on FS 64.
- **Mile 8.9**– turn right on Mountaintown Creek Trail.
- **Mile 14.3**– lower trailhead for Mountaintown Creek Trail.
- **Mile 14.9**– pass pond on right. A road enters on the right and a little further on a road enters on the left. Stay straight.
- **Mile 16.3**– turn right on paved county road #65.
- **Mile 16.9**– turn right onto gravel road which is FS 90.
- **Mile 18.5**– turn right on FS 68.
- **Mile 19.6**– finish.

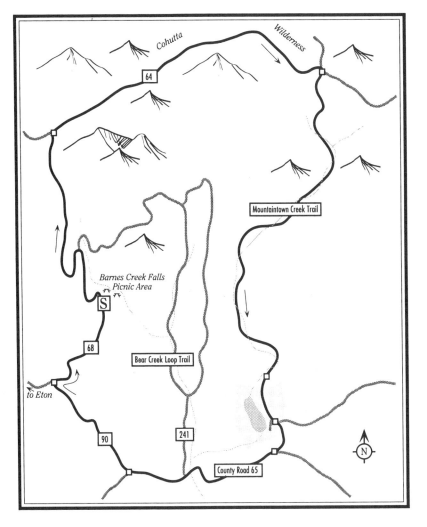

Cohutta

Wilderness

64

Mountaintown Creek Trail

Barnes Creek Falls
Picnic Area

S

68

Bear Creek Loop Trail

to Eton

90

241

County Road 65

N

MAP KEY

Bike Route........................

Forest Service Rd. #................. 419

Other Trail or Road...........

Road or Trail Name...... Rich Mountain Trail

Direction of Travel................ ⟶

Foot Travel Only............

Start/Finish............................ S

Timber Cut or Clearing..

Milepost.................................. □

Public Land......................

Other Land......................

Recreation Area...............

Major Mountain........

River, Lake, or Stream.....

3520'

2400'

1560'

Elevation Change

24

Nimblewill

Springer Mountain, the southern terminus of the Appalachian Trail, looms as you make the long climb to Nimblewill Gap. Once on top of the ridge, a rough jeep road takes you to Amicalola Falls, one of Georgia's best views.

Start/Finish

From Amicalola Falls State Park, go east on GA 52 for 6.8 miles Turn left at sign for Nimblewill Baptist Church. Go 1 mile to church. Start here.

Trail Configuration

Loop

Surface

Double track • 3.3 miles
Gravel road • 8.5 miles
Pavement • 9.9 miles

Highlights

Mountain farms, streams, waterfall, washed out road, highway, very steep paved downhill, Amicalola Falls State Park

Total Distance

21.7 miles

Time Allowance

Beginner • 4.5 hours
Intermediate • 3 hours
Advanced • 2 hours

Mileposts

- **From start**– ride west on gravel FS 28 (Nimblewill Road).
- **Mile 4.0**– road forks with gate at each fork. Bear left.
- **Mile 7.2**– Nimblewill Gap. Turn left past gate on FS 46.
- **Mile 8.3**– road forks and trail crosses. Bear left on FS 46.
- **Mile 10.5**– jct. High Shoals Road. Turn left, downhill.
- **Mile 12.0**– left at stop sign.
- **Mile 12.2**– parking lot for Amicalola Falls view. Go right.
- **Mile 13.3**– bottom of steep hill. Turn right at stop sign.
- **Mile 13.6**– turn left on GA 52.
- **Mile 17.5**– turn left on Wesley Chapel Road.
- **Mile 19.8**– turn left on GA 52.
- **Mile 20.5**– turn left at sign for Nimblewill Baptist Church.
- **Mile 21.7**– finish.

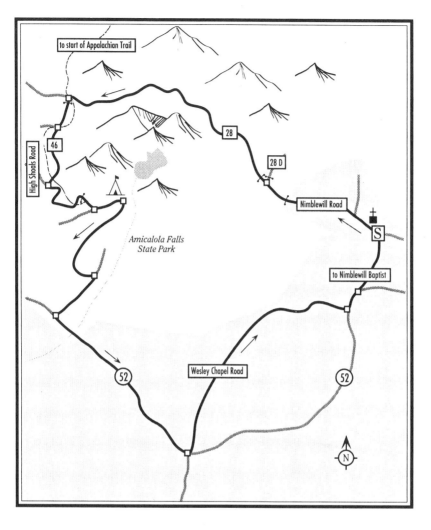

MAP KEY

Bike Route..........................
Other Trail or Road...........
Direction of Travel................ →
Start/Finish............................. S
Milepost..................................... □
Public Land......................
Other Land........................
Recreation Area...............
Major Mountain........
River, Lake, or Stream.....

Forest Service Rd. #................. 419
Road or Trail Name...... Rich Mountain Trail
Foot Travel Only.............
Timber Cut or Clearing..

Elevation Change

3200'
1734'
1500'

25

Across the TN Divide

A long steep climb takes you up to the Tennessee Divide. All the water behind you goes to the Gulf via the Chattahoochee River. All the water ahead of you goes to the Gulf via the Tennessee River. You'll cross and recross the divide before making a speedy return back down to the Hooch.

Start/Finish

From Helen, go 1 mile north on GA 17/75. Turn left on Alt. 75. Cross bridge and start at Chattahoochee United Methodist.

Trail Configuration

Loop

Surface

Gravel road • 17.7 miles
Pavement • 4.7 miles

Highlights

Great views, long strenuous climb, loose gravel, highway, river and stream crossings, waterfall

Total Distance

22.4 miles

Time Allowance

Beginner • 4 hours
Intermediate • 3 hours
Advanced • 2.25 hours

Mileposts

- **From start**– cross bridge and turn left on GA 17/75.
- **Mile 0.8**– turn right on FS 79, a gravel road.
- **Mile 3.8**– two small roads enter from right and one from the left. Stay straight on FS 79.
- **Mile 6.7**– road forks. Bear left downhill on FS 283.
- **Mile 7.3**– Indian Grave Gap. Continue on FS 283.
- **Mile 9.5**– side hike to High Shoals Falls.
- **Mile 10.8**– turn left on GA 17/75.
- **Mile 12.8**– Unicoi Gap. Just past gap, turn right on FS 44.
- **Mile 14.8**– turn left on FS 178 and go around gate.
- **Mile 18.0**– gate. Go around.
- **Mile 20**– ford river and turn left on FS 44.
- **Mile 22.4**– finish.

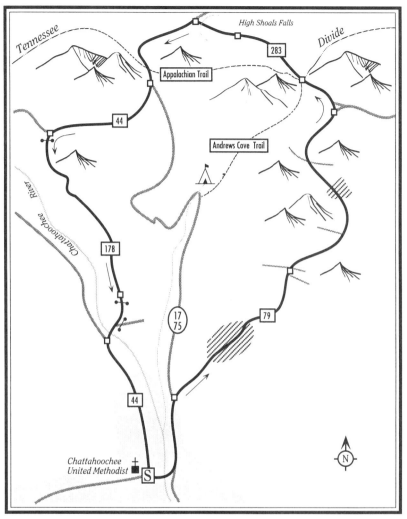

High Shoals Falls

Tennessee

Divide

283

Appalachian Trail

44

Andrews Cove Trail

Chattahoochee River

178

17
75

79

44

Chattahoochee
United Methodist

S

N

MAP KEY

Bike Route.........................		Forest Service Rd. #.................	419
Other Trail or Road...........		Road or Trail Name......	Rich Mountain Trail
Direction of Travel................	→	Foot Travel Only.............	
Start/Finish.............................	S	Timber Cut or Clearing..	
Milepost..................................	□		
Public Land.......................			
Other Land.......................			
Recreation Area...............			
Major Mountain........			
River, Lake, or Stream.....			

3355'   3200'

1500'

Elevation Change

Regional Information

Local Bike Resources
Lodging & Camping
Weather

Local Bike Resources

At the date of this printing, you will find full service bike shops are few and far between in the area of North Georgia covered in this book. It is always a good idea to be prepared by bringing your own tools and spare parts. However, if you are in need, look for:

- **Mountaintown Outdoor Expeditions (MOE)**
  P.O. Box 86
  Lower Cartecay Road
  Ellijay, GA 30540
  706/635-2524
  Sales, repair, and rental services.

- **Doug's Cyclery**
  815 B North Tibbs Road
  Dalton, GA 30720
  706/278-3775
  Sales and repair services.

Lodging & Camping

- **Mountaintown Outdoor Expeditions (MOE)**
  P.O. Box 86
  Lower Cartecay Road
  Ellijay, GA 30540
  706/635-2524
  Bunkhouse lodging in MOE-tel, camping, kitchen facilities. The well-known site of several Mountain Bowl mountain bike races every year.

Georgia State Parks

Georgia has an excellent system of state parks that not only feature recreational opportunities, but offer a wide range of overnight accommodations as well. Each park found in the North Georgia area has primitive camping, full-hookup camping, and rental cottages. Of those, several have lodges, conference centers, and restaurants. It's wise to call ahead for reservations, especially in the summer or fall leaf season.

- **Unicoi State Park & Lodge**
  P.O. Box 1029
  Helen, GA 30545
  706/878-2824 or 706/878-3366

- **Vogel State Park**
  Route 1, Box 1230
  Blairsville, GA 30512
  706/745-2628

- **Amicalola Falls State Park & Lodge**
  Star Route, Box 215
  Dawsonville, GA 30534
  706/265-8888

- **Fort Mountain State Park**
  Box 1K, Route 7
  Chatsworth, GA 30705
  706/695-2621

Camping in the Chattahoochee National Forest

There are a good number of Forest Service recreation areas located within the Chattahoochee National Forest. Each has campsites with picnic tables and many have drinking water and restroom facilities. These are open from late May through early September and sites may be taken on a first-come, first-served basis. A small fee is charged.

If roughing it is more your style, you may camp anywhere in the National Forest that is not posted "no camping". No charge or permit is required.

For a wider range of accomodations contact:

- **Dahlonega-Lumpkin County Chamber of Commerce**
  P.O. Box 2037
  Dahlonega, Ga 30533
  706/864-3513

- **Helen Business and Merchants Association**
  706/878-2521

Weather

Month	Average Temperature*	Average Rainfall
		(in inches)
January	41°	5.5"
February	43°	4"
March	50°	7"
April	60°	4.9"
May	67°	5.7"
June	75°	4.7"
July	78°	5"
August	76°	4"
September	71°	4"
October	60°	2.5"
November	50°	3.5"
December	43°	4"

All temperatures are fahrenheit. Information provided by the National Weather Service.

Notes

Notes

Notes

Notes

Notes

Notes